ARCHERY

THE ATHLETIC INSTITUTE
200 Castlewood Drive
North Palm Beach, FL 33408

Copyright © 1983 by The Athletic Institute

All rights reserved
including the right of reproduction
in whole or in part in any form.
Published by The Athletic Institute
200 Castlewood Drive
North Palm Beach, Florida 33408
Printed in the United States of America

Library of Congress Catalog Card Number 82-74329
ISBN 0-87670-086-5

TABLE OF CONTENTS

Chapter 1
From Out of the Past 3
    Through Recorded History 5
    Into the Twentieth Century 6
    Technological Advances 7

Chapter 2
Looking Over the Equipment Field 11
    Bow 11
    Arrows 14
    Quiver 16
    Protective Equipment 19
    Targets 21

Chapter 3
Choosing the Right Bow 25
    Bow Weight Chart 27
    Selection of Arrows 27
    Shaft Selection Chart 29

Chapter 4
Preparing To Shoot 33
    String the Bow Safely 33
    Basic Shooting Position 34
    Start With Your Stance 34
    Nocking the Arrow 35
    Determine Your Eye Dominance 37

Chapter 5
Hand Positions and the Draw 41
    Putting It All Together 43
    Geometry of the Drawing Arm 47

Chapter 6
Establish Your Anchor 51
    High Anchor 51
    Low Anchor 53
    String Alignment for Steady Form 54

Chapter 7
Ready for the Aim and Hold 59
    Aiming With a Bowsight 59
    Aiming Without a Sight 61

Chapter 8
Developing Your Hold....................................67
    Drawing Tension and the Release......................68
    Follow Through......................................70
    Breath Control Is Important 70

Chapter 9
Practice and Scoring 75
    Practice on the Home Target Range....................75
    Tests for Greater Accuracy 75
    Troubleshooting 76
    A Scattered Pattern?................................76
    Scoring 76

Chapter 10
Competitive Archery....................................81
    Sources of Official Rules 81
    Silhouette Shooting 81

Chapter 11
Safety Rules..87
    Safe Arrow Removal.................................87
    Inspect Your Tackle 89
Glossary 91

v

A WORD FROM THE PUBLISHER

THIS SPORTS PUBLICATION, is but one item in a comprehensive list of sports instructional aids, such as video cassettes, 16mm films, 8mm silent loops and filmstrips which are made available by The Athletic Institute. This book is part of a master plan which seeks to make the benefits of athletics, physical education and recreation available to everyone.

The Athletic Institute is a not-for-profit organization devoted to the advancement of athletics, physical education and recreation. The Institute believes that participation in athletics and recreation has benefits of inestimable value to the individual and to the community.

The nature and scope of the many Institute programs are determined by a Professional Advisory Committee, whose members are noted for their outstanding knowledge, experience and ability in the fields of athletics, physical education and recreation.

The Institute believes that through this book the reader will become a better performer, skilled in the fundamentals of this fine event. Knowledge and the practice necessary to mold knowledge into playing ability are the keys to real enjoyment in playing any game or sport.

Howard J. Bruns
President and Chief Executive Officer
The Athletic Institute

D. E. Bushore
Executive Director
The Athletic Institute

FROM OUT OF THE PAST

From Out of the Past

Babylonian boundary marker (1098 - 1081 B.C.). (Courtesy British Museum)

One of the many mysteries of prehistory is who invented the bow and arrow. It is thought, by reason of the latest archaeological evidence, to have first appeared in the Solutrean period of the Late Stone Age, some 45,000 to 50,000 years ago.

However, the beginnings of the bow are not as important as its influence in human evolvement. It has long been classed, with the control of fire and development of the wheel, as one of the greatest of man's early discoveries. It marked his first successful attempt at storing energy. It is impossible to determine which came first, the fire drill or the bow and arrow. But it is reasonable to assume that whichever came first, the other developed from it. It is also within reason to speculate that competitive shooting at a mark, as in a form of bowhunting practice, was likely man's first sport.

The role of the bow in history extends from early in man's development across many thousands of years, and its story is not yet finished.

The bow, through all time, has assumed four basic forms — the longbow with straight ends, the short bow, the composite recurve and the "Johnny-come-lately" compound bow. There are many variants and shapes of these forms. They can be further classed as basically of two kinds — wooden and composite. The wooden ones were either self bows (of a single piece of wood) or were strengthened by the attach-

3

ment of woven animal sinews, such as early Eskimo bows.

Early composite bows were formed of wood, horn, antler, bone, sinew, baleen and gut in various combinations. They of course are not as ancient as the self wood bow, but even so were undoubtedly used some 30,000 years ago. The finest composite bows were developed in Europe and Asia, whereas the wooden bow was the weapon of African, South American and South Pacific natives. The bows of early North American Indian tribes were of both types.

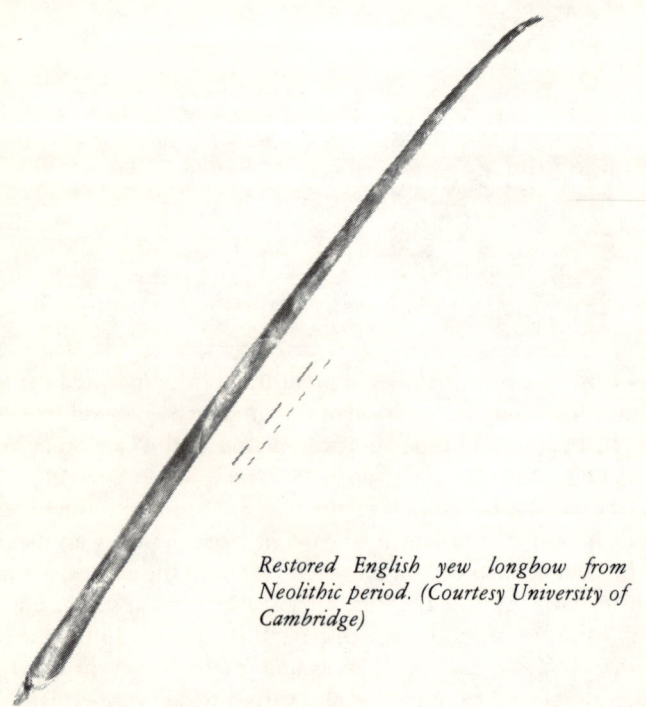

Restored English yew longbow from Neolithic period. (Courtesy University of Cambridge)

A longbow is most simply defined as a bow that is long rather than short, the length being equal to or greater than the height of the archer. The majority of ancient longbows were six feet or more in length.

The typical longbow is of a single piece of wood, such as yew or elm, with a deep D-sectional shape, the ratio between depth and width being not less than 4 to 5. At the arrow plate the bow is wider than at any other place on the top limb. There is no concession in this design to allow the arrow to pass near the center of the vertical plane of the

From Out of the Past

limbs. No arrow rest was built into or attached to the bow, the arrow being shot across the top of the forefinger of the bow hand.

Through Recorded History

In western Europe the longbow was at its peak during the 14th and 15th centuries. By 1650 the early development of firearms had eliminated the bow as a weapon of war. From then on the longbow was solely a sporting arm. In 1653, Thomas d'Urfey wrote: "Let Princes therefore shoot for exercise. Soldiers to enlarge their magnanimities. Let Nobles shoot 'cause 'tis a pastime fit. Let Scholars shoot to clarify their wit. Let Citizens shoot to purge corrupted blood. Let Yeomen shoot for the king's and nation's good. Let all the Nation's archers prove, and thus we without lanthorns may find virtuous men."

A medieval archer with longbow.

Longbows are still being produced and used both for target competition and for bowhunting. Modern versions, however, often employ laminated construction such as layers of bamboo or facing and backing

Archery

of fiberglass to enhance their strength, prevent stringfollow, and prolong their life.

Early composite bows reached their pinnacle of efficiency and performance in Mongolia, Turkey and Persia during the 12th, 13th and 14th centuries. These bows were short (for use by cavalry), highly reflexed, and the best were composed of animal sinew backing and water buffalo horn facing over a wood core. The English longbowmen had been invincible in battle until they met mounted Saracen archers during the Crusades, at which time they were thoroughly outclassed by the better range, power and maneuverability of the bowmen of Islam.

When the English and other Europeans began to flood into the Americas, they found bowhunters and archer warriors everywhere. These contacts, combined with the memory of ancestral bowmen, led to a gradual growth of archery interest here, and in turn led to development of the modern composite bow.

In the 18th and 19th centuries, archery was more of a fashionable pastime for the gentry than an organized sport. The modern age of American archery began with the formation of the United Bowmen of Philadelphia in 1828. The twenty-five club members secured their longbows and accessories from England and those were used as models for others made by the members. For a time, other clubs sprang up in imitation of the UBP, but the Civil War (1861-65) put an end to organized archery for many years.

Following that conflict, the writings of Maurice Thompson, recounting the archery adventures of him and his brother, Will, caused a resurgence of interest in the sport and when the American National Archery Association was formed in 1879, Maurice served as its first president.

Into the Twentieth Century

Moderate activity continued until after World War II, when scientific technology came into the picture. Engineers tested all sorts of new materials, ever trying for better balance and precision.

During this same period the bowhunting adventures and subsequent writings of Dr. Saxton Pope and Arthur Young, and a bit later the shooting exploits of Howard Hill and Fred Bear, added impetus to the archery revival. The bowhunting phase was then, and continues to be, the largest segment of American archery but its popularity has also greatly influenced the growth of competitive target archery as well.

Another big boost to the latter aspect came in 1972 when archery, after a long absence, was once again established as a Gold Medal sport in the Olympic Games. This not only resulted in tremendous growth

From Out of the Past

at the high school and college levels in America, but also in many countries around the world.

In 1967 the first U.S. Intercollegiate Archery Championship was held. Now more than 65 colleges and universities compete annually in this event. The Junior Olympic Program of the National Archery Association and the new emphasis on lifetime sports also contributed to its growth.

A production stage in a modern archery workshop.

Technological Advances

As archery interest grew, so did innovative skill in bowmaking. Many methods, some centuries old and some new, were tried. Sinew, silk or hickory was used as backing to aid in resisting tension, while osage orange, fiberglass and aluminum were used to resist compression. A few of the other woods used in bow construction have been yew, maple, ash, lemonwood, greenheart, elm, red cedar, mulberry, juniper and hickory. Limb ends evolved from static or non-working recurves to working recurves. In the latter the limb ends bend or "unwind" as the bow is drawn, thus adding their own energy upon release, resulting in smoother shooting and superior arrow cast.

The majority of present-day target bows have working recurve limbs and formed, comfortable handle risers cut away to allow passage of the arrow near the center of the bow. This window also provides for placement of a bowsight and gives the archer a clearer view of the target.

The most efficient bow limb design yet developed, actually an

Archery

adaptation of the ancient Turkish or Persian composite, consists of fiberglass backing and facing over core laminations of hard maple. This is in place of the sinew backing and horn facing of the earlier bowyers.

Modern target archery is a highly developed sport, as specialized as golf, and calls for precision shooting at fixed ranges. The bow's tradition, its world-wide history, and the romanticism with which it is surrounded, are known to no other sport. It offers the ideal combination of fun, physical fitness and family togetherness. It can be as competitive or as leisurely as one chooses and is one of the few sports that offers ideal recreation for both men and women and all age groups.

LOOKING OVER
THE EQUIPMENT FIELD

Looking Over the Equipment Field

Successfully introduced by an unrecorded ancestor, bow equipment has evolved from primitive necessity to engineered reliability. Perhaps no other single piece of man's ingenuity has been subjected to such a long span of evolution. Though modern equipment still holds to the basic shape and relies on the exact method of propulsion; (i.e., the released energy stored in a taut string) nothing about the gear is untouched by modernization. Change began when someone replaced the bent limb tied by a vine with animal horns strung with sinew. Innovation continues to this day and if the alterations are more exact and complicated, the motivation remains identical — improvement.

Today manufacturers can certainly claim to offer something for every archer. Sizes, shapes, materials and prices can all be accommodated with an ease that truly makes archery a sport for everyone.

Consistent with the wide assortment of equipment is the need for such variety; archery is an individual sport that requires personal selection. Bow and arrow, while universal in appeal and interest, are weighted and sized for specific archers. Belief that "one size fits all" could be the most dangerous safety violation associated with this sport.

While individual size and strength make sizing a personal task, this book will offer several charts and graphs which will help you determine your basic equipment needs. Remember, however, it is best to consider advice from a knowledgeable source to ensure a precise match. Selected wisely, the lightweight, sturdy equipment available to today's archers will provide years of safe family fun.

Archery equipment is commonly referred to as "tackle." The tackle required for target archery consists of a bow, matched arrows, a quiver for carrying the arrows, a shooting glove or finger tab and an arm guard. Other accessories such as an arrow rest and bowsight are also available and, while not essential, they are important for serious archers.

Bow

As the biggest, most important and expensive piece of equipment in the sport, much care and consideration should go into proper selection of the bow. A bow not powerful enough will quickly discourage an archer interested in constant improvement. On the other hand, a bow too powerful can make archery enjoyment impossible as well as potentially dangerous.

With the assortment and variety of equipment available, no one should have trouble finding the right bow to meet any need.

Bows are generally made of laminated fiberglass and wood or solid

Archery

fiberglass. Both types have characteristics which should be considered in making a selection.

Cutaway view of a laminated bow.

For beginners, many experts recommend solid fiberglass bows. These bows are sturdy and reliable and hold up very well to rough treatment. They are very forgiving of weather and under normal conditions and with minimum maintenance will last indefinitely. They are also less expensive and make an ideal choice for someone interested in beginning archery.

The laminated variety, on the other hand, is more expensive than the solid limb bows. However, this extra expense provides a bow which delivers arrows with more speed and with increased smoothness — both important considerations to serious archers.

There are several types of bows to choose from. Again, proper selection should be determined generally by what you want to use the bow for — hunting or target shooting.

The longbow, made famous by English archers and best dramatized by Robin Hood's expertise, is a straight instrument. Many archers enjoy the long, clean lines of this classic bow and combined with modern laminated manufacturing, it is enjoying a resurgence of popularity.

Developed after the straight or longbow, the recurve has largely dominated modern archery. These bows are available in a variety of sizes and costs. Elegant and attractive, recurves combine pleasing physical appearance with a smooth pull.

The recurve is recommended for students because it is inexpensive and is the type commonly used in interscholastic competition.

One of the newest innovations in archery tackle, the compound bow, was introduced less than 20 years ago. These bows are made in either one piece full-length style or in a take-down style, with handle sections of either hardwood or metal alloy. They employ a system of eccentric wheels or pulleys connected by steel cable to each other and to the bowstring, which produces a block and tackle-like advantage.

The result of this design is that as the bowstring is drawn, resistance increases as with a conventional bow until mid-draw is reached. At that

Looking Over the Equipment Field

point the eccentric wheels roll over and resistance to your pull decreases. At full draw you will be holding 15 to 50 percent less than the actual thrusting power of the bow. In other words, peak pull is at mid-draw rather than at full draw. As the bowstring moves forward from release therefore, the poundage increases to peak and then decreases, giving

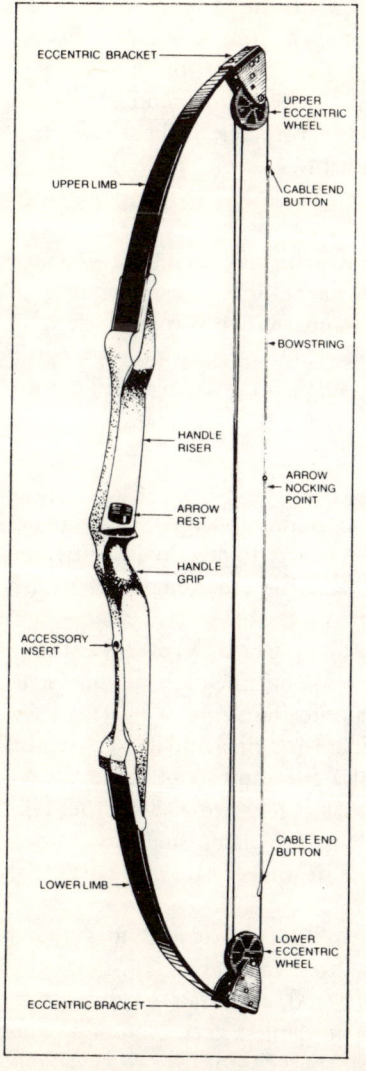 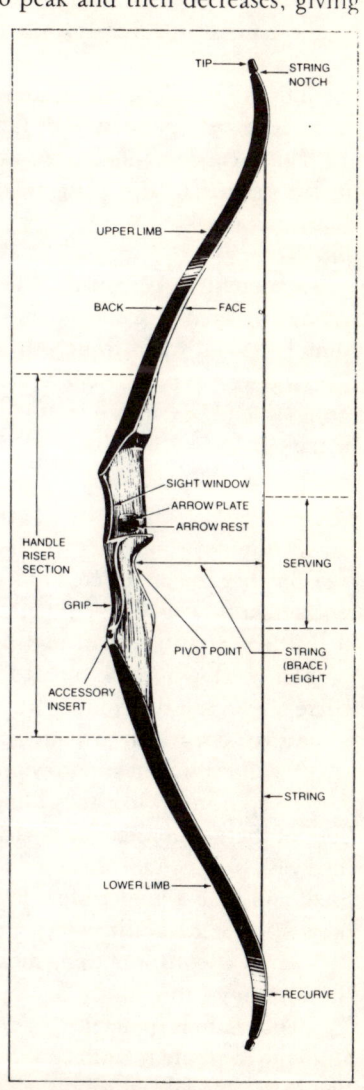

Compound bow and its parts   *Modern recurve bow.*

13

Archery

a major increase in foot-pounds of energy for direct application to the arrow. Not only is energy output increased, but the bow is much easier to hold at full draw during aiming. The advantages of easier holding plus greater energy output and thus greater arrow velocity with flatter trajectory, have made it possible for women and youngsters to better handle bows of medium to heavy draw weights.

Compound bows are not at the present time sanctioned for national or international target competition. However, they are allowed for and are very popular with field archers and bowhunters.

No discussion about bows would be complete without considering the string. The first string was probably a simple vine, later replaced by animal skin. While these "strings" were effective, they were unreliable.

Modern strings are made of Dacron or Kevlar with an area — center serving — coated with nylon or monofilament. Strings are sold in lengths from 23" to 74" and from 8 to 20 strands. When you purchase your bow, it is wise to purchase several extra strings to ensure proper length. Strings should be checked carefully before shooting and replaced if worn or frayed.

Arrows

Performance in archery means understanding something about arrows for they too are offered in a wide variety to meet many different requirements. The different parts of the arrow are the nock, fletching or feathers, cresting, shaft and point.

The nock is a small, molded plastic tip which fits over the string. There are several different types of nocks, but the most popular style is the snap-on, which actually snaps onto the string.

The fletching on an arrow provides wind drag and also causes the shaft to spin much like the rifling of a gun causes a bullet to rotate. Both of these actions are necessary for accuracy. Arrows are either fletched with plastic vanes or natural feathers. The plastic vanes are weatherproof and have a longer life. However, feathers create more drag and provide greater stabilization.

Arrow cresting is nothing more than a series of colorful rings around the shaft used to identify one arrow from another.

The shaft is generally made of wood, fiberglass or aluminum, although some are manufactured out of stainless steel, graphite or carbon glass. Specialized solid shafts, for sport fishing, are also available and are made of fiberglass or aluminum.

When selecting your shafts, you should consider the merits of each and weigh them against your particular need. Wood shafts are generally

Looking Over the Equipment Field

the least expensive and are more expendable, usually an important consideration for beginning archers.

Fiberglass arrows are generally the heaviest, and therefore fly with a greater arching trajectory. While these shafts are more expensive, they resist warping and are sturdy unless mistreated.

Aluminum arrows are completely weatherproof, are light to provide an even flight path and are consistent in weight and stiffness. While the aluminum shafts can develop warps, many sporting goods stores have arrow straighteners which can straighten them for a nominal fee.

Effective archery also calls for a knowledge of tips, or points. There are many different arrowheads and each is designed for a specific archery need. Field points of simple steel are ideal for target shooting

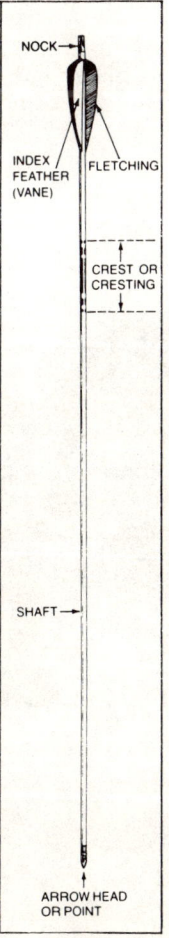

The parts of an arrow.

15

Archery

while razor-sharp broadheads are used for hunting. The point you use, again, will be determined by the specialized requirements of your sport.

The student archer should be sure the arrows are the proper length and are matched to the bow and to each other. All arrows in a set should have the same weight (usually within five grains) and same stiffness, or "spine." The stiffness must be suitable for the bow which will propel them or the arrows will not fly accurately. No amount of practice will ever overcome the built-in flaw of mismatched equipment. Equipment must be closely matched for consistently reliable flight.

Quiver

Preference, demand and intent are the overriding considerations in choosing a quiver because, like other aspects of archery, the arrow carrier has developed a multiple personality. All quivers will carry arrows, so the choice will be made according to personal needs.

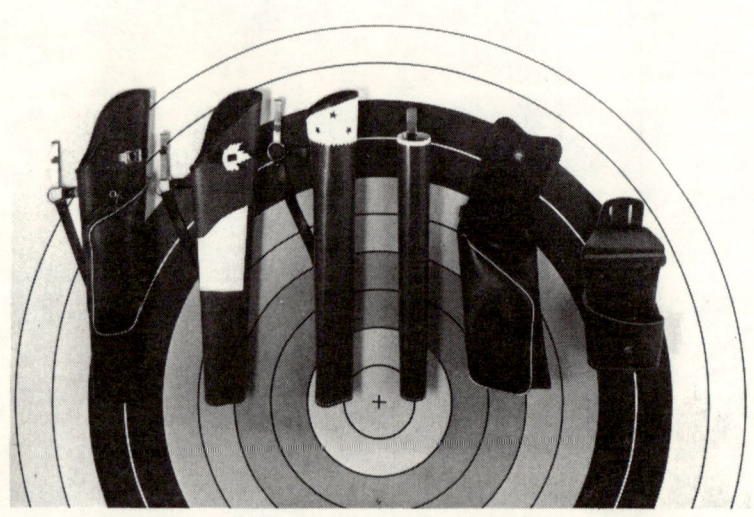

Quivers come in a wide variety.

Looking Over the Equipment Field

When it comes to target shooting, the most widely used quiver is the side, or hip quiver. This is usually an open tube which allows easy access to your arrows. The hip quiver attaches to your belt and most models have pockets for storing accessories. When used for hunting, the hip quiver usually holds six to eight arrows snugly in rubber clips and generally features arrowhead caps to protect archers from the sharp edges of broadheads.

For archers shooting indoors, a very popular quiver is the pocket quiver. This is a simple leather or plastic quiver which slips into a rear pocket. This is adequate, as necessary equipment need not be carried on the archer.

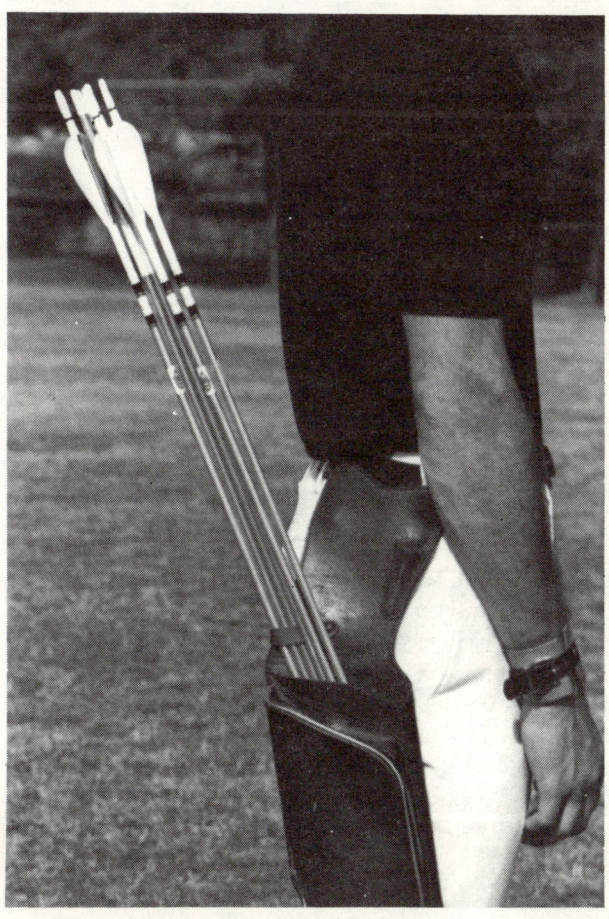

Hip quiver attaches to belt.

17

Archery

For certain type target rounds, like the metric 900 or American, the ground quiver is an ideal choice. The ground quiver is an arrow rack, generally with a sharp spike on one end, which is pushed into the ground. Most ground quivers, which are ideal if the archer is going to fire repeatedly from one spot, also have a place to hold the bow when the archer goes to retrieve arrows.

Perhaps the quiver most people think about when they consider archery equipment is the back quiver. This is the quiver used by American Indians and Robin Hood. This quiver is still popular among hunters and target shooters. However, many archers no longer use the back quiver because of these limitations.

For example, during hunting arrows are not held apart by the back quiver and noise may become a factor. Also, it is possible to ruin the fletching on bushes or undergrowth. For target shooting, many archers find it cumbersome or awkward to reach over their shoulder to get or replace arrows.

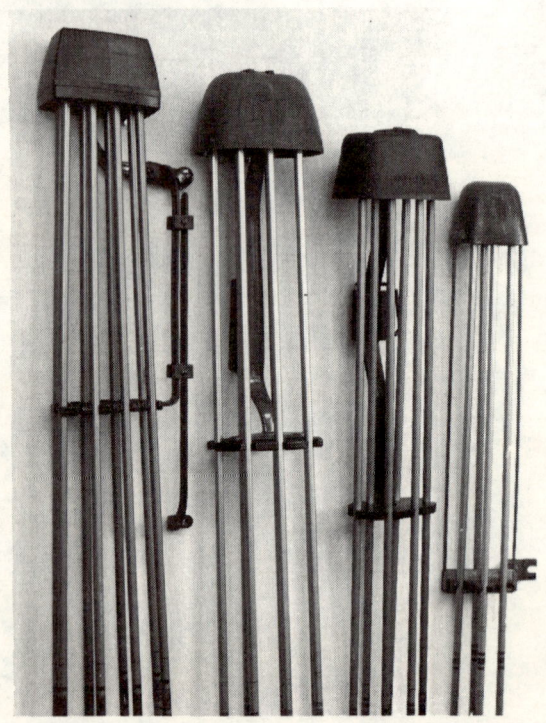

Bow quivers feature caps for safety.

Looking Over the Equipment Field

Most bowhunters use a bow quiver which holds four to eight arrows and attaches directly to the bow. The arrows are held snugly in place with rubber or plastic clips and most have rugged sturdy arrowhead caps to protect against accidents. The bow quiver offers hunters the advantage of increased mobility through trees and brush.

Protective Equipment

Archers should always use protective equipment on their fingers and arms. Not only does this eliminate discomfort, but it also permits a smooth and unimpeded release of the arrow.

For the fingers, archers may want to use either the tab, the glove or the release-aid. Whichever you use, finger protection is essential if the archer is to avoid blisters which will lead to discomfort and a poor release.

The tab is a small leather or smooth vinyl device which usually covers the first three fingers with a slot for the nock. Tabs come in a variety of shapes and are sized to fit any finger. Selecting the proper size and style will be a matter of individual choice.

Shooting gloves also come in a variety of styles and sizes. Gloves fit snugly over the first three fingers and offer an adjustable wrist strap

Equipment for finger and arm protection.

Archery

to ensure comfort. Generally, the tab contributes to a somewhat smoother release while providing a little less protection than the glove. The glove may take a little time to get broken in and to fit comfortably, but provides more protection.

Another method of protecting fingers is a newer innovation called the release-aid. This is a mechanical device which actually holds the nocked arrow for the archer. While release-aids offer the advantage of smooth release because of reduced friction, these devices are not allowed in many tournaments. Indeed, a special unlimited class has been developed for those archers wishing to use this shooting accessory.

It will take an archer only one slap on the forearm with a bowstring to develop an appreciation for an armguard. The armguard is a must. It protects the arm from the string slap (which occurs every time the arrow is released properly) and will prevent the string from catching on clothing and ruining the shot. Armguards come in various sizes for target, hunting, or field and may be of leather or synthetics.

The majority of armguards are about six inches long and three inches wide, though they are available offering protection all the way from the biceps to the wrist. For novice archers the armguard is essential.

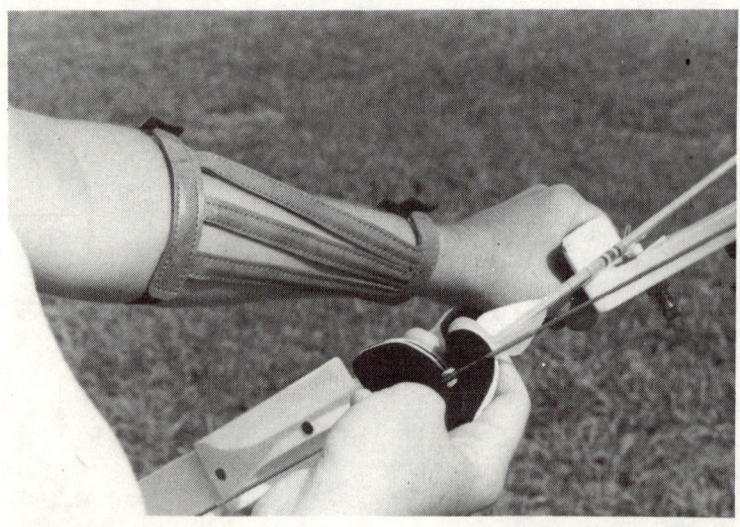

Armguard and finger tab in use.

Looking Over the Equipment Field

Targets

Archery target matts, called butts, may be made from a variety of materials. The kind most commonly used in tournament archery consists of wound and stitched grass. These are firm enough to stop the arrow in flight and still permit its easy withdrawal. Plastic foam matts also are available and some field-type ranges use baled excelsior.

For actual targets to shoot at, only the imagination limits the variety. There are novelty targets such as dart boards, bingo, animals, baseball, etc. For hunters, there are countless animal targets available.

Whichever target you use, make sure your target butt is large enough to stop any arrow which misses the mark.

Target faces are attached to the butts. The traditional target face consists of ten rings and five colors, ranging outward from the bull's eye in this order: gold, red, blue, black and white. This provides for two rings of each color and scoring is counted, by rings, starting at ten for a bull's eye and ranging out to a score of one for the outer ring.

Novelty targets are fun to use.

CHOOSING THE RIGHT BOW

Choosing the Right Bow

Once you initiate an interest in this sport, you have to answer the archery riddle: Which comes first, the bow or the arrow?

While it would seem that the bow is the logical answer, many experts would disagree. They argue that arrow draw length will actually determine which size bow you will ultimately need.

Whichever of these two essential items you choose first, to ensure a proper selection often requires professional advice. Your archery supplier or coach can provide knowledgeable help.

In selecting a bow there are many factors to consider including your size, strength, intention and, of course, price. While these variables can only be answered individually, there is some basic information anyone can use to ensure correct tackle.

Bows must accommodate your draw length. To determine this length there are two popular methods.

The first method is to place the end of a yardstick up to your chest — about level with your shoulders. While holding the yardstick between your fingertips, stretch your arms forward. The arrow length you need will be approximately one inch longer than your fingers reach.

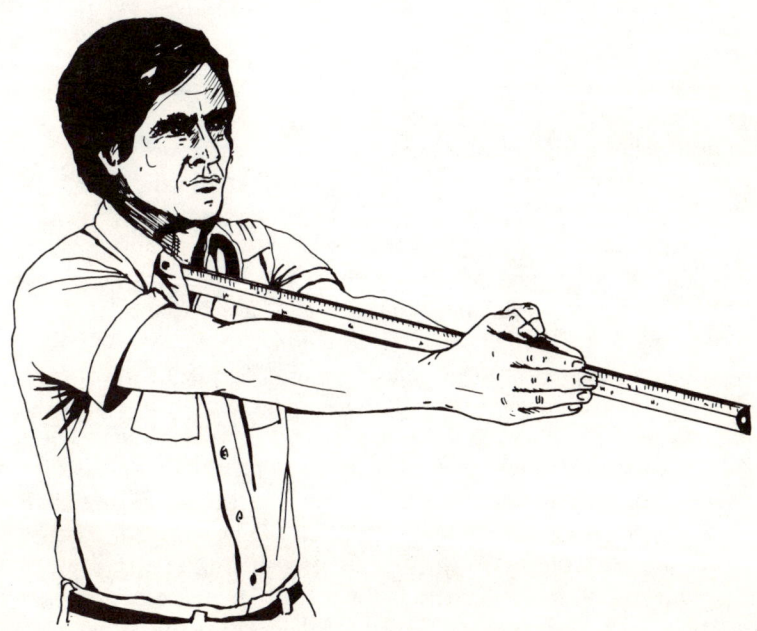

Easy method to determine draw length.

Archery

While this is not exact, it will provide the novice a fairly accurate starting place in considering archery tackle.

Using meauring arrow (marked off in inches) to find draw length.

The second method is more accurate and is preferred by experts. In this method, an archer actually draws a bow and arrow into a firing position while someone measures to the front of the arrow shelf, which is part of the arrow rest. This method provides exact draw length and should be utilized if possible. Be sure to use a very light-weight bow so you will be able to hold a full draw to get an accurate measure.

Another important point about bow selection is that all recurve and longbows are weight rated at 28″. This means that a 30 pound recurve will actually take 30 pounds of holding weight at a 28″ draw. If you have a shorter or longer draw, the holding weight will change. Seasoned archers usually figure that each inch greater or less than 28″ will add or subtract two pounds to the holding weight, although in heavier bows this weight difference will be greater.

Compound bows are also marked for ease in selection. A bow marked 28-30″ draw and 40-55 pounds can actually be adjusted to a draw between 28 and 30 inches with the weight altering accordingly.

One mistake many archers commonly make in getting their first bow is selecting a bow too powerful for them. Remember that while you may be able to draw a powerful bow once or twice in a store, it

Choosing the Right Bow

is not the same as shooting an entire day. Too much bow will cause discomfort and make accuracy impossible. The American Archery Council has stated that a 55 pound bow can stop any North American game animal. In choosing a bow, make comfort a consideration. After you develop shooting strength, a more powerful bow might be in order.

Bow Weight Recommendation Chart

	20 lb. & under	20 lb.	25 lb.	30 lb.	35 lb.	40 lb.	40 lb. & over
Children 6-12	X	X					
Teen (Girl)		X	X				
Teen (Boy)		X	X	X			
Ladies — Target		X	X	X			
Men — Target				X	X	X	
Hunting							X

According to standards of the Archery Manufacturers Organization (AMO)

Selection of Arrows

So you have your bow. The proper weight and length. Now, once again you have decisions to make that must be keyed to one thought — matching your arrows to your bow.

Arrows must be the correct weight and length to provide safe and accurate shooting.

As noted, the first place to start in arrow selection is to determine the proper draw length, which is defined as the distance you draw your arrow back before you fire. To find this length, measure from the bottom of the string groove in the nock to the back of the bow at full draw.

Personal draw length will be influenced by physical size, the length of your arms and the spot to which you anchor during your draw.

To find your draw length, begin with a bow that you can easily draw back. This will allow you to loosen up your muscles and find a comfortable anchor spot. Once you are loose, draw the bow with an extra-long arrow on it into your anchor point. Have someone mark the shaft at the back of the bow. Then measure from that mark to the bottom of the nock and you will have an accurate draw length.

For target arrows, the correct length will be between ½ to 1 inch longer than the point where the arrow rest contacts the shaft. For hunting arrows, which take a longer head, the distance must be increased.

Archery

After you arrive at the proper length, you must select arrows that have the correct stiffness — or spine — to match your bow. For this selection, arrow manufacturers have charts available at archery outlets which will give you shaft sizes designed to fit the weight of your bow.

The reason for the importance in this match is so the arrow will not wobble as you shoot. This fluctuation would result in decreased accuracy. Beginners should ask for help to make sure the proper match is made.

Shaft Selection Chart

RECURVE BOWS — The left-hand column shows the actual weight of your recurve bow. Follow the horizontal line that shows this weight over to the correct arrow length. In this box are listed the recommended shaft sizes, with the most widely used sizes printed in bold type.

COMPOUND BOWS — Determine the equivalent compound bow weight by adding the peak and holding weights and dividing by two. Use this figure and the left-hand column, as described for the recurve bow.

Use the right-hand column if you know both the compound peak bow weight and the percentage of let-off. Find the peak bow weight under the proper let-off column and follow the horizontal line back to the box under the correct arrow length. (See the Quick Reference Chart on page 29.)

Shaft Selection Chart

To determine the compound equivalent bow weight, add the peak and the holding weights and divide by 2.

"QUICK REFERENCE" CHART

ACTUAL RECURVE BOW WEIGHT — OR — EQUIVALENT COMPOUND BOW WEIGHT (POUNDS & KILOGRAMS)	COMPOUND PEAK BOW WEIGHT (POUNDS & KILOGRAMS) 30% LET-OFF	COMPOUND PEAK BOW WEIGHT 50% LET-OFF	CORRECT ARROW LENGTH 24" 61.0 CM	25" 63.5 CM	26" 66.0 CM	27" 68.6 CM	28" 71.1 CM	29" 73.7 CM	30" 76.2 CM	31" 78.7 CM	32" 81.3 CM
20-25# (9.1-11.3 KG.)	24-29# (10.9-13.2 KG.)	27-33# (12.3-15.0 KG.)	1416⊙	1516⊙	1516⊙ 1518⊙	1518⊙ 1614⊠ 1518⊠	1616⊙ 1713⊠ 1518⊠	1714⊠ 1716⊙ 1813⊙	1813⊙ 1814⊠ 1816⊠	1913⊙	
25-30# (11.3-13.6 KG.)	29-35# (13.2-15.9 KG.)	33-40# (15.0-18.1 KG.)	1516⊠	1516⊙ 1518⊙	1518⊙ 1614⊠ 1616⊠	1616⊙ 1618⊠ 1713⊠ 1714⊠	1616⊙ 1618⊙ 1713⊠ 1714⊠	1716⊠ 1813⊠ 1814⊠	1816⊠ 1913⊙	1914⊠ 1916⊠	
30-35# (13.6-15.9 KG.)	35-41# (15.9-18.6 KG.)	40-47# (18.1-21.3 KG.)	1516⊙ 1518⊠	1518⊙ 1614⊠	1616⊙ 1618⊙ 1713⊠ 1714⊠	1616⊙ 1714⊠ 1716⊙ 1814⊠	1716⊙ 1813⊠ 1814⊠	1716⊙ 1816⊠ 1913⊠	1816⊠ 1913⊙	1914⊠ 1916⊠	2016⊙ 2114⊠
35-40# (15.9-18.1 KG.)	41-47# (18.6-21.3 KG.)	47-53# (21.3-24.0 KG.)	1518⊙ 1614⊠	1616⊙ 1618⊙ 1713⊠	1618⊙ 1714⊠ 1716⊙ 1813⊠	1716⊙ 1714⊠ 1814⊠	1718⊙ 1816⊠ 1914⊠ 1916⊠	1818⊙ 1914⊠ 1916⊠	1818⊙ 1916⊠ 2013⊠ 2014⊠	1916⊠ 2016⊠ 2114⊠	2018⊙ 2114⊠ 2115⊠ 2213⊠
40-45# (18.1-20.4 KG.)	47-53# (21.3-24.0 KG.)	53-60# (24.0-27.2 KG.)	1616⊙ 1618⊠ 1713⊠	1716⊙ 1714⊠ 1716⊠ 1814⊠	1716⊙ 1714⊠ 1814⊠ 1813⊠	1716⊙ 1816⊠ 1814⊠	1718⊙ 1914⊠ 1916⊠	1818⊙ 1914⊠ 1916⊠	1916⊙ 2013⊠ 2014⊠	1918⊠ 2016⊠ 2114⊠	2018⊙ 2115⊠ 2213⊠
45-50# (20.4-22.7 KG.)	53-59# (24.0-26.8 KG.)	60-67# (27.2-30.4 KG.)	1618⊙ 1716⊠ 1813⊠	1718⊙ 1816⊠ 1813⊠ 1814⊠	1718⊙ 1816⊠ 1913⊠	1718⊙ 1816⊠ 1914⊠ 1916⊠	1818⊙ 1914⊠ 1916⊠	1818⊙ 1916⊠ 2013⊠ 2014⊠	1918⊙ 2016⊠ 2114⊠	2018⊙ 2114⊠ 2115⊠ 2213⊠	2117⊙ 2216⊠
50-55# (22.7-24.9 KG.)	59-65# (26.8-29.5 KG.)	67-73# (30.4-33.1 KG.)		1718⊙ 1816⊠ 1913⊠	1818⊠ 1914⊠ 1916⊠	1916⊙ 2013⊠ 2014⊠	1916⊙ 2013⊠ 2014⊠	1918⊠ 2016⊠ 2114⊠	2018⊙ 2114⊠ 2115⊠ 2213⊠	2117⊙ 2216⊠	2216⊙
55-60# (24.9-27.2 KG.)	65-71# (29.5-32.2 KG.)	73-80# (33.1-36.3 KG.)			1916⊠ 2013⊠ 2014⊠	1918⊠ 2016⊠ 2114⊠	2018⊙ 2114⊠ 2115⊠ 2213⊠	2018⊙ 2115⊠ 2213⊠	2117⊙ 2216⊠	2216⊙	2219⊙

NOTE: 1413 NOT LISTED, SHOULD BE USED FOR DRAW LENGTHS OF LESS THAN 24" (57.6 CM) AND BOW WEIGHTS UNDER 20 LBS.
⊙ INDICATES XX75®   ⊠ INDICATES X7®
2024 ALLOY (24SRT-X®, SWIFT® & GAME GETTER®) NOT LISTED = 1# STIFFER IN SPINE & 1# LIGHTER IN WEIGHT THAN XX75®
XX75® X7® 24SRT-X® SWIFT® GAME GETTER®   *Reg. TM. Jas. D. Easton, Inc.
© Copyright 1981 Jas. D. Easton, Inc.

PREPARING TO SHOOT

Preparing To Shoot

String the Bow Safely

WARNING: STRINGING THE BOW WITHOUT A STRINGER IS DANGEROUS.

Use of bowstringer eliminates slipping.

Sure, you've seen archers slip the bow behind their leg and manually bend it over and loop the string over the tip. What you haven't seen are the times when the string has slipped off, causing the archer to suffer a potentially dangerous blow to the face or eyes.

The older methods of stringing bows, namely the "step-through" and "push-pull" techniques, are no longer valid. They both involve potential harm to either the archer or his bow, which is completely eliminated by the use of a simple cord bowstringer. The latter device is very inexpensive, weighs just a few ounces, and is easy and fast to use, particularly for women and youngsters. In our age no archer should be without one of these accessories.

The bowstringer is simply a length of strong cord with end pockets of leather. With the lower bowstring loop in place on the lower bow

Archery

nock and the upper loop slipped on over the bow limb, the end pockets of the bowstringer are fitted over the bow tips. It is then a simple matter to stand on the center of the cord, pull the bow up at the handle with one hand, while the other hand slides the upper string loop into place on the bow nock.

Basic Shooting Position

In most sports there are maverick performers who do well with unorthodox form. This is also true in archery. But for assured success and consistency in performance, good shooting form is essential. Once learned and practiced regularly, good form is your best guarantee of early mastery of the art and consistently high scores.

Start With Your Stance

There are three basic stance positions: the "Square," "Open" and the "Closed." The pictures below show these three positions. The "Closed" stance is not recommended, since it fosters string interference with the body and tends to promote an out-of-line bow shoulder. The most popular position is the slightly open stance, where the foot closest to the target is slightly drawn back from square and the trunk of the body is slightly open to the target. Usually each archer will develop a stance that fits his or her physique and often it will be somewhere

Square stance.   *Open stance.*

Preparing To Shoot

between the square and open stances. Weight should be evenly distributed on both feet and centered over the arches. Do not concentrate weight on your heels or toes. The feet should be spread about shoulder width apart but never closer than twelve inches. Once you have found a comfortable stance make it a regular habit. Stand erect. Good basic posture will contribute to consistent shooting performance and will build confidence and a positive attitude.

1. Feet and shoulders slightly less than perpendicular to the target.
2. Feet about shoulder-width apart.
3. Stand erect with weight evenly distributed on both feet.

Nocking the Arrow

Holding the bow in the bowhand (left hand for right-handed persons, reverse for "lefties"), grasp the arrow by the nock end and lay it across the arrow rest. Now the right (or draw) hand may set the nock onto the bowstring with the cock feather, or vane, on the arrow pointing directly away from the bow. See photograph.

The arrow should be nocked between 1/16'' and 3/16'' above 90°. An arrow nocked too low will tend to wobble or "porpoise." One nocked too high will result in a poor flight and cast. A permanent nocking

Closed stance   *Slightly open stance.*

Archery

point on the bow string is the best assurance of consistently correct positioning of the arrow. Many archers make a nocking point by wrapping the string with dental floss or other thin thread and covering it with rubber cement or glue. To find the proper spot you may use a bow-square at your dealer. This will give you the ideal nocking point.

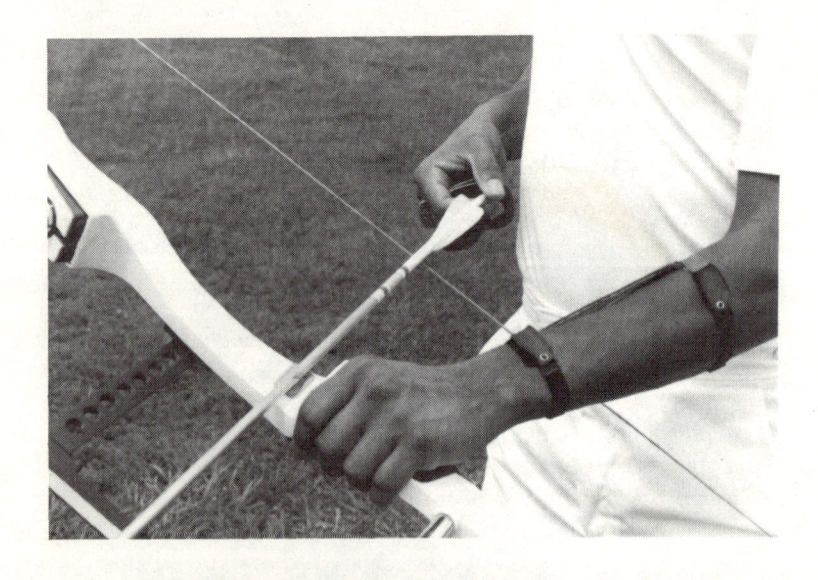

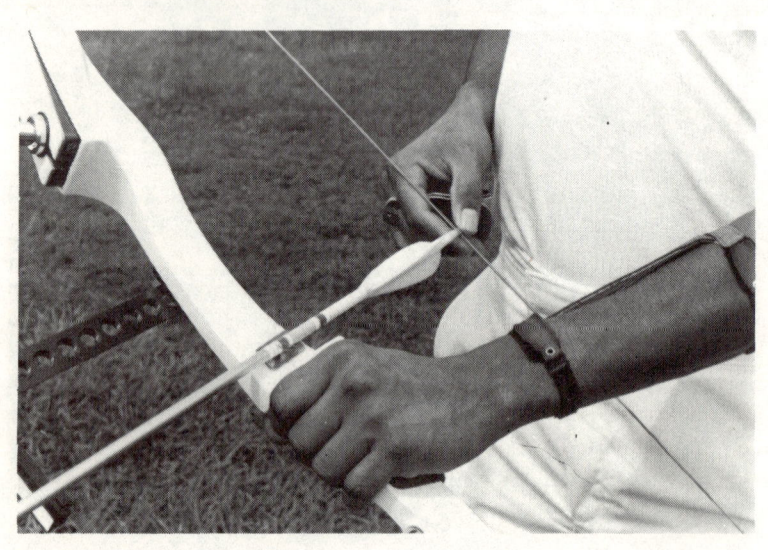

Two steps in nocking the arrow.

Preparing To Shoot

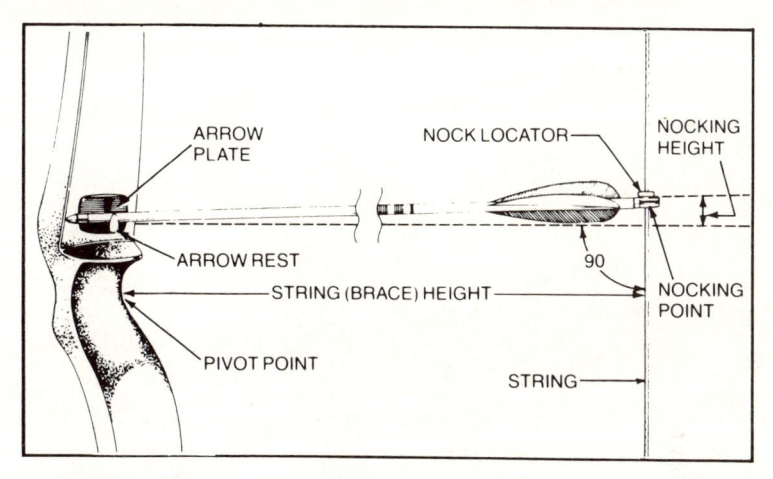

Nocking area of bow.

Determine Your Eye Dominance

Eye dominance is a factor sometimes overlooked in learning to shoot a bow. In most other daily activities this makes little difference, but it is quite important in the process of proper sight alignment in archery. Many beginners start off using correctly matched equipment and proper form, yet cannot seem to properly group their arrows. The cause can often be traced to an improper sighting picture. Anyone, for example, who is right-handed but whose left eye is the dominant eye, may have trouble simply because of not being able to line up his shots where he is looking. The dominant or master eye should be the one aligned with the arrow shaft for best results.

It takes only a second to determine which is your dominant eye. Extend your arm and point your forefinger at some object across the room. Then close the left eye. If the finger still is centered on the object, your right eye is the master eye. If the object is in line when the right eye is closed, the left eye is the stronger.

So, if your left eye happens to be the master eye, even if you do most everything else right-handed, you should learn to shoot the bow left-handed.

HAND POSITIONS AND THE DRAW

Hand Positions and the Draw

After nocking the arrow, place three fingers on the bowstring with the arrow nock between the index and second fingers. The string should lie in the groove of the first joint of the three fingers. The fingers should curl well around the string before starting the draw.

It is important to keep the back of the hand and wrist flat and not cupped (see picture). The thumb and little finger should curl toward the palm. As you apply tension to the bowstring, the force of the draw will tend to straighten the draw fingers slightly, keeping the arrow on the arrow rest. If the arrow falls off the rest, check to see if the back of the hand is still lying flat and make sure it is not cupped and that the fingers are still curled around the string at the start of the draw. Do not pinch the nock. It will remain on the string without any special support.

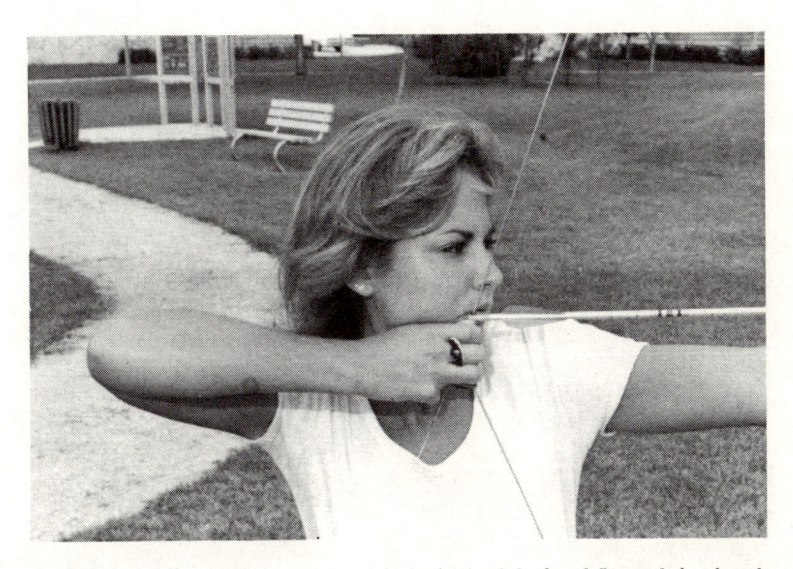

Curl fingers well around the string, with the back of the hand flat and the thumb and little finger curled toward the palm.

Archery

There are a number of variations of the bow hand position during the draw and all are acceptable to various coaches. The important point to bear in mind is the need to hold the bow during the draw and release so the least amount of "torque" is transmitted from the hand to the bow. Torque is any pressure not in a direct line from the elbow of the draw arm to the center of the target. This should be done with maximum comfort and minimum strain.

1. The grip should never be tight. The fingers of the bow hand may be closed loosely around the bow, but you should be careful not to tighten them. A bow sling allows the archer to keep his fingers open during the shot.
2. The back of the hand should lie flat, in line with the forearm as nearly as possible. This position is the subject of some debate but it will help you to remember that the central idea is to prevent torque. A sharp break in the line of the wrist will cause torque, as will a wrist locked in an awkward position.
3. The bow arm should extend toward the target and a slight pressure should be exerted with the draw arm. This will permit you to seat the bow hand before the draw. Any attempt to position the bow hand during the draw will almost certainly result in torque.

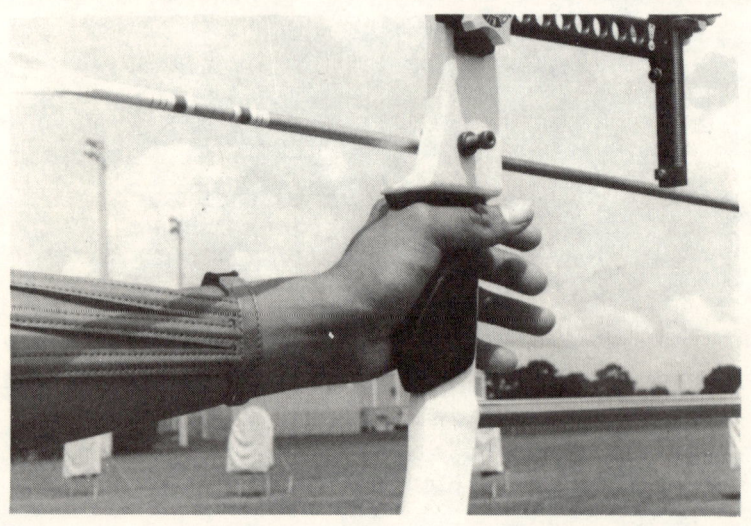

Fingers of bow hand are closed loosely around the bow.

Hand Positions and the Draw

The draw should be a very simple movement. Remember: It is important to keep everything in a straight line. The draw action should be slow and steady. The archer should feel that all forces are focused on the center of the target.

Putting It All Together

Now we will apply the lessons we have learned about the stance, proper hand positions and nocking the arrow.

Take the correct stance at the shooting line — slightly open position, erect posture and looking directly at the target. The head should be in the same fixed position for each shot; it should not move during the draw or while shooting. While maintaining slight tension on the string with the draw hand, raise the bow arm to the proper level for the shot. On level ground this will be at about shoulder level. At this point you should check your bow hand for correct position and make sure the elbow of the bow arm is pointing to the nine o'clock position.

During the shot the head must remain stationary. The eyes should be constantly on the target. This concentration is essential for consistency. The only time you should violate this rule is if you sense you are making a mistake in your form.

Raise the bow to shoulder level.

Archery

After you have nocked the arrow, have assumed a comfortable stance and are prepared, there are three different methods to draw the bow.

The first two methods are almost identical. Starting with bent arms, the archer pulls back his right arm while the bow arm is pushed outward to a locked position; thus both arms share the work of the draw.

Pull back on drawing arm.

Correct position with bow arm locked.

Hand Positions and the Draw

The only variation between the first two draws is that in one the archer starts with the bow in a low position and it is raised as he draws. This is an upward draw.

In the other draw, a downward draw, the bow is raised above the head and, as the arms extend, the bow is lowered into correct firing position.

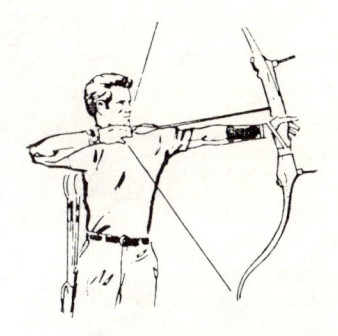

Both of these methods provide the archer with a smooth draw. Since both hands share the work of the draw, there is less tendency for the arms to weaken, making it easier to hold correct form and aim.
The downward draw may be better for an archer who keeps ending up in a hunched position when drawing upward and it may be easier to use with a heavy bow.

Archery

Another type draw is the "T" draw. In this style the archer raises the bow to firing position, actually aiming on target. From this position the archer completes the draw entirely with the drawing arm. While this method offers the advantage of constant sighting, it requires greater strength to ensure a clean, smooth motion throughout the draw.

Whichever draw you use, the archer should strive for consistency. During the pull of the string only the arms and shoulders should move. The body should be erect and stationary.

Position head and raise the bow.

Aiming on target.

Hand Positions and the Draw

Geometry of the Drawing Arm

At full draw, a line projecting backward from the line of flight should intersect a point at the lower part of the elbow. In other words, the drawing arm should follow a plane **very slightly** above the line of the arrow.

A flat, unbroken line should extend from the first joint of the drawing fingers along the back of the hand and wrist and along the outside of the forearm while the fingers remain comfortably curled around the string. The fingers act as a hook and the wrist is merely the linkage between the forearm and the fingers. The draw is actually made from the elbow, with as little tension as possible between the elbow and fingers.

Position at full draw.

ESTABLISH YOUR ANCHOR

Establish Your Anchor

The anchor is the point on the face or jaw to which the drawing hand pulls the bowstring before releasing. It is essential that the anchor is secure enough so that the archer will always draw to the same position. It usually consists of more than one contact point. There are two basic anchors used in archery, the high and low anchors. Although there are variations of each, we will discuss only the traditional high and low anchors. Usually the low anchor is used in target archery when shooting with a sight. The high anchor is associated with instinctive (or "bare bow") shooting without a sight.

The importance of this anchor point is easily explained. In shooting a rifle, the amount of force driving the bullet is constant. Each shell has carefully controlled grains of powder to ensure the same charge for each shot.

In archery the energy which propels the arrow comes from the string. If the string is pulled tighter, it will drive the arrow with more force. Thus, to ensure constant firing energy, the archer must have a spot, or anchor, to which to draw.

Another reason a constant anchor position is important is in aim. Rifles and hand guns have front and rear sights. To ensure proper elevation, the two sights are aligned.

While many bows have sighting devices, they do not have a backsight. To get the same angle on each shot requires the archer to pull the string to a constant anchor spot. Correcting your aim and improving your marksmanship will be impossible unless you establish a consistent anchor from which you can make necessary shooting adjustments.

High Anchor

To establish the high anchor, the archer draws the string to the side of the face. The forefinger lies along and just below the cheek bone. The tip of the finger extends to or near the corner of the mouth. (Remember: The drawing fingers are still curled comfortably around the string.) The thumb lies under the jaw bone, against the neck, with

Archery

the web between the thumb and forefinger cradling the hinge of the jaw beneath the ear. The thumb must be curled into the palm so it will lie under the jaw without interfering with the anchor. If the head and hand are in the correct position, the arrow will lie directly under your eye and you will be sighting over the arrow, directly along its line of flight.

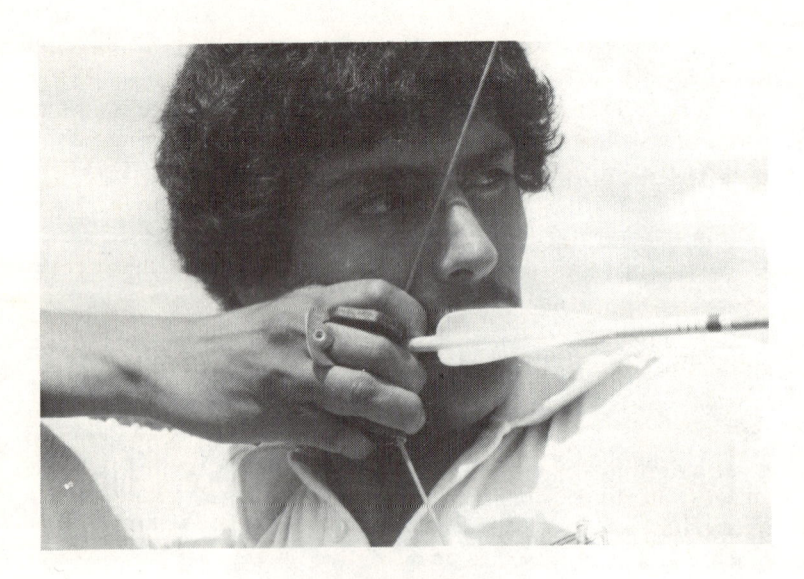

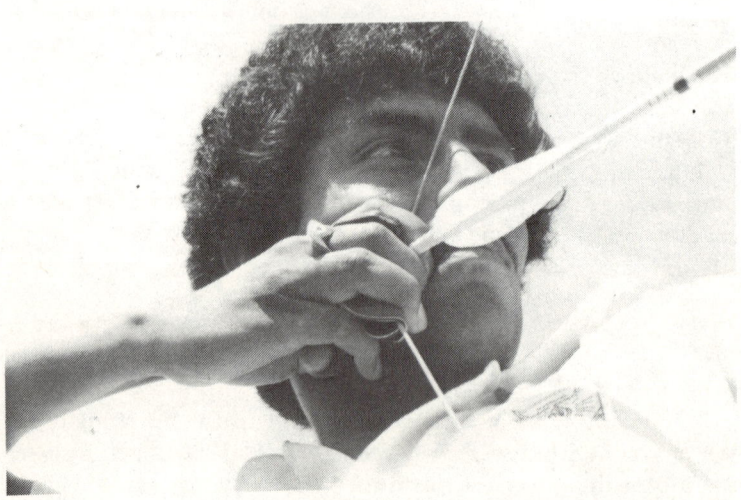

The high anchor with forefinger under cheekbone, fingertip at corner of mouth. Arrow shaft is directly under master eye.

Establish Your Anchor

Low Anchor

This anchor is preferred by most target archers because its lower location in relation to the eye allows sight settings higher on the bow for greater distance. Also, the contact points are more precise for most archers, assuring greater accuracy. The draw is made to a point under the face with the curled forefinger resting firmly under the chin. The

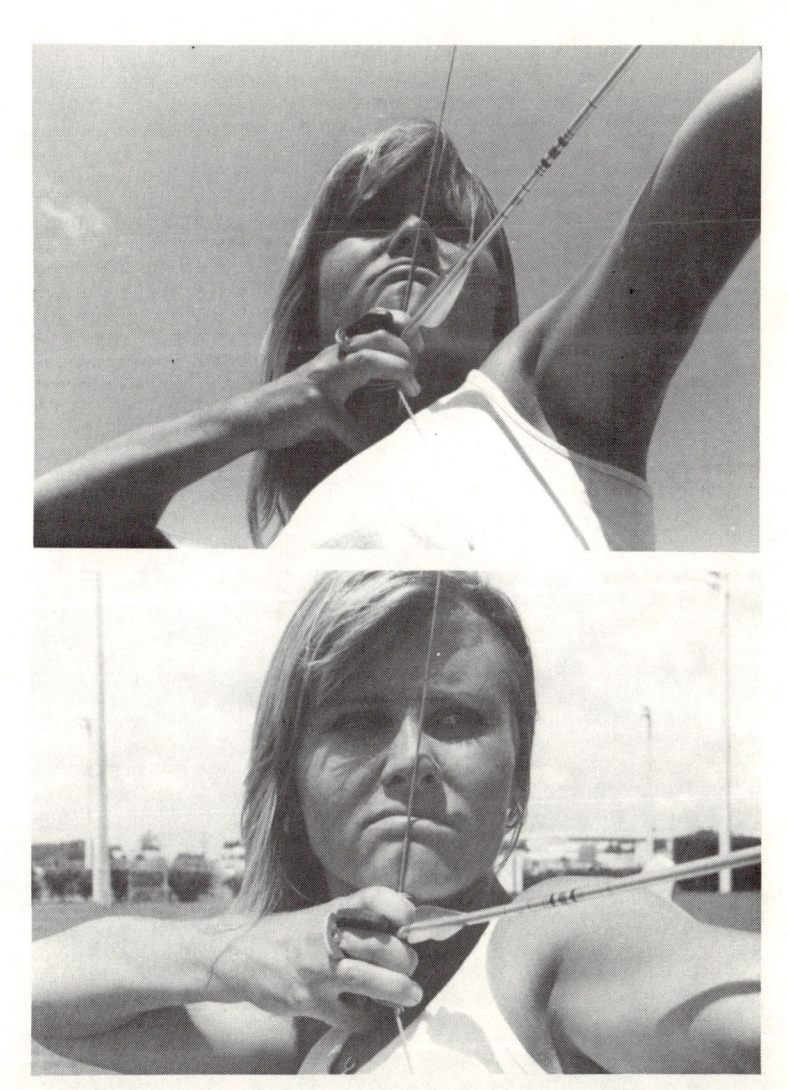

The low anchor with curled forefinger resting firmly under chin. String centers on tip of nose.

Archery

string bisects the center of the chin, centering on the tip of the nose. Many archers actually touch the nose. The physical build of the archer may have some effect on this point.

Although it is best to develop a secure, natural anchor, many people find the kisser button an essential aid. The kisser button is attached to the string and adjusted so it will touch the archer's lips to ensure a consistent anchor point. Many archers feel this button gives them another check to ensure a proper anchor.

String Alignment for Steady Form

In both the high and the low anchors, it is necessary to align the string. This is important in order to keep the head in the same position each time the bow is drawn.

In the case of the high anchor, the alignment is usually accomplished by noting the blurred image of the bowstring in front of some portion of the master eye. As long as it is kept in the same relative position to the eye, the alignment is accomplished. Some archers align the string image with a portion of the bow, making aiming even more precise. However, in the case of the high anchor with the position in front of the eye, the archer is usually using the arrow itself as an aiming aid.

In the case of the low anchor the archer is often utilizing a bowsight and is not using the arrow as an aiming aid. Since the sight is some distance from the arrow, it is necessary to be absolutely sure that the

When the master eye is focused on the target, the string will appear blurred.

Establish Your Anchor

relationship between the head, the sight, and the arrow is the same with each shot. Therefore, the string must be aligned with the same definite point on either the bow or the bowsight for each shot.

In a brief amount of time string alignment will become automatic. However, it is an important item of form and should become part of the mental checklist for each shot.

Remember — forefinger under chin, string aligned with center of chin and nose.

READY FOR THE AIM AND HOLD

Ready for the Aim and Hold

At this point, if your form is good, you're ready for the next two areas that need emphasis for accurate shooting: the aim and the hold.

There are two basic aiming techniques that archers use — instinctive aiming or bowsights. While, of course, both have merit in different situations, there is a constant that the archer must follow regardless of aiming method. When preparing to shoot, the archer must concentrate the aim in the center of the target.

Keeping your attention riveted to the center of the mark is archery's answer to "keep your eye on the ball." In order to be an effective archer, you must block out all other objects.

That is why shooting position and form are so important. Once you're on the firing line, the basics should be secondary. Your concentration should be focused on one thing only. You must focus precisely in the center, not just near it or passing through it.

The hold is another area that requires special attention. Not only must you be sure that a full draw is maintained, but you must pause before loosing the arrow. While more technical elements of the hold will be discussed, it is appropriate to consider the importance of getting a bow that does not overpower you. A proper hold is impossible if the archer is struggling to pull the string to the shooting anchor.

Aiming with a Bowsight

Bowsights may be as simple as a pin taped to the back of the bow or as complex as the most expensive mechanical sighting instrument available. But it all boils down to a dot fixed on the target. The method of setting this dot and calibrating its movements determines, to a large extent, its cost and effectiveness.

While no one can determine if you will prefer shooting with a bowsight or if you will be effective without one, it should be noted that almost every target archer uses some form of bowsight. It's a precision sport demanding concentration on form, practice and control. Consistent scores require the use of a sight.

Another reason most target archers use a sight is because they are shooting from fixed distances. Since bowsights are set by distance, knowing the length between archer and target makes bowsights very effective. The use of a bowsight seems to be the easiest method for most beginners to achieve satisfactory shooting results.

Most commercial bowsights have an adjustable pin that can be set to predetermined distances. The sight pin is used to line up targets from the various shooting spots.

Archery

For instance, one pin setting may be for 10 yards, the second for 20 yards and the third for 30 yards. When shooting from an uneven distance, the archer merely aims between settings. For example, during a 25 yard shot, the aiming point would be midway between the 20 and 30 yard pin settings.

Many bow hunters also rely on bowsights. Most hunting sights are

Bowsight lines up target with precision.

One of the most popular types of bowsights.

sturdy and simple, with a series of pins that are also preset by the hunter for various distances. Since hunters will not be in situations where they know exact yardages for shots, the pins are used as reference points. Again, these pins are used to help the hunter aim. Once the approximate distance is determined, the archer adjusts his aim accordingly. Many hunters have also found that it helps to put a small drop of different colored paint on each of the pins. This color code makes it easier to locate the correct sight pin in a hunting situation, where speed and accuracy are critical factors.

Once you have made your selection, you will have to sight-in your bowsight. With the sight in a given position, a flight of two or three arrows is shot, carefully noting the position of this group in relation to the target center. Now the sight pin should be moved from the center to the arrow cluster. In other words, if the arrows are low, the sight should be moved down. If they are to the left, the sight must be moved left, and so on. Once the sight position is determined, it should remain unchanged for that distance providing there is no change in the form or weather conditions. Most sights provide calibration markings — or a place for them — so the archer can mark off the various distances for future reference.

It's necessary, of course, to know the distance you are shooting before releasing the first arrow so the sight can be set. Otherwise you may waste several arrows just to determine the proper sight setting. Once the bow is "sighted in," there should be no appreciable change in the setting. Even when changing arrows, one adjustment should serve for all settings.

Extreme concentration should be used to keep the sight in the center of the target. It must be locked in there, not just passing the center. It takes a conscious effort to keep it settled throughout the shot.

Once you have sighted in your bow and have mastered the basic shooting techniques, you should be able to achieve consistent arrow groupings. If you find trouble grouping your arrows, it might be an indication that they are out of alignment.

Aiming Without a Sight

The high anchor usually is employed for this type of aiming because it brings the arrow closer to the eye and the angle between the line of sight and the line of flight is closer than with the low anchor. In order to understand the various methods of sighting used by most instinctive, and/or "bare-bow" shooters, it will be helpful to explain the term, "point of aim."

Archery

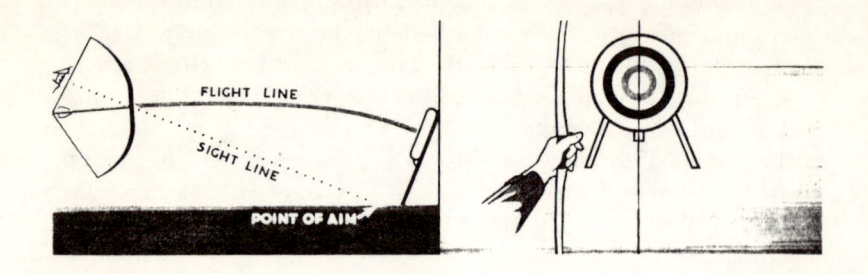

Relationship of flight line to sight line and point of aim.

You will notice that for your sight line to be on the target, the distance to the target is quite far. In most cases, the sight line over the point of the arrow will be below the target. This explains why many bare-bow shooters anchor at a point quite high on the face. Some even place all three fingers **under the arrow nock** so their line of sight is almost identical with the arrow's line of flight. In such cases, the archer is using the tip of the arrow as a sighting device. This is an effective style but it requires exact knowledge of the distance to the target.

Another method is sometimes called "gap shooting." The archer is aware of the arrow tip in relation to the target but sees it in so-called "secondary vision" and is conscious of the position of the point without looking directly at it. This is not as definitive as "point of aim" but it has the advantage of an unchanging anchor and doesn't require moving the drawing fingers in relation to the arrow nock. This method is really the subconscious aid that many "instinctive" archers use without realizing it.

True instinctive shooting involves many subtle factors. It calls for a good perception of trajectory much like a baseball or football player needs for throwing to a target. Your mental computer has to calculate the distance to the target and such critical elements as trajectory, wind speed and direction, the terrain (uphill or downhill), etc. Some archers develop an uncanny talent for doing this and it contributes to their shooting success, especially at hunting.

Most archers are able to shoot quite well without a sight using some of these methods; perhaps a little of each. In order to shoot without a sight, begin practicing from a distance which will permit you to aim directly at the target. A large target is recommended to spare you the drudgery of retrieving arrows that miss the mark. Practice at close range until you can group your arrows together, then gradually increase the distance in increments of five yards. Soon you should be able to judge

Ready for the Aim and Hold

your ability to shoot without a sight and decide if this is the method for you. Remember: As in shooting with a sight, it is necessary to concentrate on the center of the target.

8

DEVELOPING YOUR HOLD

Developing Your Hold

It's important to hold the full draw long enough to perfect the aim and to reach the proper tension before releasing the arrow. When the archer concentrates on the target his aim should settle on the center, providing his form is correct. During this aiming process it will be necessary to hold the bow at full draw. Many beginning archers think they are holding at full draw only to discover they are "creeping," that is, releasing the tension ever so slightly, permitting the arrow to move forward on the rest.

The time required to hold will vary from archer to archer, but even two full seconds can seem like an eternity. Five seconds or longer is not unusual for a top tournament archer. Bear in mind, however, that too long a hold will result in fatigue and loss of control. Should this occur, it's best to let down and begin again.

Archer at hold position.

Many beginning archers make the mistake of failing to develop a proper hold. They draw back and release the arrow the moment the full draw is reached. From an accuracy standpoint, this will produce inconsistency.

Even seasoned archers sometimes develop this condition, which is called "target shyness." To correct this problem, you must remember to pause once you have a full draw.

Practice pulling to a full draw, aiming, and then relaxing the draw

Archery

without shooting. This exercise will force the archer to pause before firing. Again, the importance of a proper-sized bow cannot be overemphasized. If you cannot develop a proper hold, perhaps you should consider using a less powerful bow.

Drawing Tension and the Release

There is a joke that tells a story about a man who has a tiger by the tail but he needs help to let it go. A full drawn bow is not unlike the tiger. Once you have completed the draw and aim, and have assured yourself that your form and concentration are satisfactory, it would seem that the simplest thing to do would be to fire, or loose the arrow.

But actually the release of the arrow is one of the most common trouble spots for most archers. Improper tension or finger action at the time of release causes most difficulty.

The tension problem is called "creeping," that is, allowing the arrow to move forward on the rest. The way to cure creeping is to increase the drawing tension while keeping the drawing wrist, forearm and hand (excepting the three string fingers) relaxed.

Creeping is a tension problem.

Another common error is called "plucking" the string. This results from jerking the hand away from the face to release the string instead of the smooth release.

A third fault is tightening the drawing fingers before release. They should remain well-curled around the string, but no additional tension should be felt during the hold. Tightening them can push the ar-

Developing Your Hold

row off the rest or result in a poor release, inaccuracy, or even sore fingers. Remember: All these errors in releasing the arrow reduce accuracy. You can improve technique and accuracy by being more relaxed, more natural in your shooting.

Rather than a definite action, the release is a reaction to the hold and aim. As the aim is perfected and the drawing tension is maintain-

A jerking motion results in string plucking.

Practice relaxing finger muscles for smooth release.

Archery

ed, the archer need only relax the muscles controlling the fingers. The string will pull itself out of the fingers smoothly and the drawing hand and forearm will react backward. Once you learn to release by relaxing the drawing fingers, the action will become smooth and almost subconscious.

The release must be a definite and controlled act of will so that everything is physically and psychologically ready for the shot. Don't allow the release to become so automatic that it happens before all the elements of form and aim are ready.

Follow Through

As in all sports, the follow-through is critical. This means, simply, that the aim and form are maintained after the release, preferably until the arrow reaches the target. This will assure that form and aim are not abandoned before completing the shot. Failure to follow through can result in a breakdown of the aim-and-hold procedure before the arrow is released.

1. Aim: Concentrate on aiming until the arrow strikes the target. Don't break form and try to watch the **arrow**. Concentrate on the target.
2. As the bow hand moves forward, the drawing arm moves backward. Hold this position until the arrow reaches the target.

The follow-through maintains form and aim.

Developing Your Hold

Breath Control Is Important

There is one final area that should be considered. Breathing is an element of accurate shooting that is often overlooked. In many finesse sports breathing is very crucial. But in archery it is even more so because the anchor position is on the face and breathing motion may cause the facial muscles to move. Though it can be argued that the movement will be slight, the distance between target rings is also very slight.

While every archer will find a method of breath control that suits him, one very common style has been copied from the U.S. Army rifleman's manual.

In this method the archer takes a deep breath and exhales, then follows with a half-breath which is held through the draw, aim and release.

*PRACTICE
AND SCORING*

Practice and Scoring

Practice on the Home Target Range

As in the development of most skills, a progressive type of archery practice is best.

Eventually you will be able to comfortably shoot a hundred or more arrows in a session, but not until the necessary muscle build-up has taken place.

Start with just two or three at a time in a series of 10 to 15. Begin at a close range of 10 yards or so, then move out, adding distance and number of shots as you progress from day to day.

For indoor short-range practice, batts can be set up in a basement or garage. In the interests of safety, block all entrances and hang a rug or heavy fabric backstop behind the target, a little way out from the wall, to prevent arrow damage or deflection. There are also nets designed for this purpose.

Outdoor range distances are only limited by the size of your backyard. Set up in an area where safety procedures of ensuring lots of open space or the use of substantial butts and a backstop can be followed.

Tests for Greater Accuracy

After the basic principles of archery have been mastered and you have practiced extensively with your chosen combination of bow and arrow, it is time to think of refining your techniques.

Here is a simple method of determining needed adjustments in your arrow flight. Shoot five or six arrows at eye level, standing about 10 yards away from the target. Observe how the arrows hit the target and at what angle.

A perfect flight, shot with the rest and nocking point aligned, will show only the nocks on the end of the arrows when viewed straight on. If the arrows have entered at an angle with nock ends up, move the nocking point down; if they have hit with nock ends low, adjust the nocking point upward.

Another test for flight accuracy is to shoot into a frame covered with paper. Stand about 5 feet away and shoot at a 90 degree angle from the ground. The hole made in the paper will tell you what corrections need to be made by the direction of the tears. The perfect shot will leave only a hole the size of the shaft and slices showing where the fletching entered.

Archery

Troubleshooting

Once you have begun shooting, you should find that practice will cure most accuracy problems. However, the following are common areas that often trouble the beginner:

Shooting to the Left
1. Grip on the bow may be too tight.
2. Anchoring too far to the right of your eye and shooting left.
3. Release may be jerky, resulting in a sharp pull of the bowstring to the right at the time of release. Learn to relax on all shots.
4. Arrows may be too stiff for the bow. If you continually shoot to the left, ask an experienced archer to try your bow. He can advise you on your tackle.

Shooting to the Right
1. Arrows may be too limber. Check with an experienced archer.
2. Bow grip may be moving to the left after release. Use a little firmer grip.
3. Might be collapsing. Be sure of follow-through and keep bow arm at center of target through the shot.

Over- or Under-Shooting
1. Check release and anchor point. You may be releasing the arrow from a point too far above or below your anchor.
2. Bow arm may be dropping. This is a common error. Be sure to keep both hands in shooting position until the arrow is well on its way to the target.

A Scattered Pattern?

No beginning archer will have a very close pattern at the start. But if your arrows continue to scatter unreasonably around your targets and you cannot bring them together, you probably have developed a number of poor shooting habits. Study the fundamental techniques illustrated in this book and resume practicing. If you cannot improve your pattern ask a skilled instructor to study your technique.

Scoring

Three to six arrows shot successively constitute what is called an **end** in archery. In field archery an end may be four or more arrows. Different archery rounds require a different number of shots per "end," (or turn). At the completion of each "end" the arrows are scored and retrieved.

In target archery each ring on the target represents a scoring value.

Practice and Scoring

The **gold** circle in the center of the target is called the "bull's eye." Each colored ring radiating out from the bull's eye has a different scoring value.

Should an arrow cut two colors, the higher of the two values is scored. An arrow which strikes outside the target in the white petticoat area does not score. An arrow which hits a target other than the proper one quite obviously is not scored at all.

A score is based on the proper number of arrows for an end only. Should an extra arrow be shot by mistake, the highest scoring arrow is not counted.

As soon as the value of the arrows is recorded, the archer should return to the area behind the shooting line to total his score. This is an act of courtesy and will speed up the shooting.

COMPETITIVE ARCHERY

Competitive Archery

Archery competition is conducted in rounds. Generally, a round is defined as the completion of a series of specified shots with a given number of arrows from specified distances. The usual procedure is for each contestant to shoot a fixed number of arrows from the farthest distance, moving up to the next shooting position closer to the target. Rounds may vary in distances and the number of arrows from each position.

Sources of Official Rules

Presently, those organizations which concern themselves with competitive archery on a national scale are the National Archery Association, the National Field Archery Association and the Professional Archers Association. For information concerning rounds and rules you may contact these organizations at the following addresses:

National Archery Association (NAA)
1750 East Boulder Street
Colorado Springs, Colorado 80909

National Field Archery Association
31419 Outer I-10, Route 2, Box 514
Redlands, California 92373

Professional Archers Association
731 North Cliff
Sioux Falls, South Dakota 57103

American Archery Council
200 Castlewood Drive
North Palm Beach, Florida 33408

Silhouette Shooting

A new addition to archery for hunters and nonhunters is silhouette shooting, one of the fastest growing shooting sports in the world today. Shoots are sponsored by well-known organizations, many of which have been formed strictly for the purpose of furthering the sport. Bowhunters' silhouettes are an adaptation of this fast-growing shooting sport.

Recently an international organization was formed specifically for bowhunters. It is designed to provide competition and fellowship by utilizing and developing the skills and equipment used in bowhunting.

This is not target archery. Silhouette shoots provide a fun outing for participants and nonparticipants alike, as well as contribute toward the lasting skills of the bowhunter.

The possibilities found in silhouette shooting are endless. What's more important, the benefits of silhouette shooting are much the same for the archer as for the firearms buff — the targets and distances are representative of actual hunting conditions; the targets respond immediately to a solid hit by falling over; and spectators as well as shooters can share in the excitement of the sport.

In the rifle and pistol sports, four basic silhouettes are employed: chicken, pig (javelina), turkey and ram. The targets are made of steel. The grade and thickness depends on the type and caliber of ammunition used.

For bowhunters, special arrow-receptive ethafoam silhouettes built to international standards of shape and dimension have been developed.

Silhouettes are standard in shape and dimension.

You may ask, "Why not different silhouettes for the bowhunter?" The silhouette shapes are based upon international acceptance and standardization of the existing four silhouettes of chicken, pig, turkey and ram. For the bowhunting sport to grow and hold an international position there must be a great deal of crossover from the rifle and pistol sports. A bowhunter walking into a gun store wearing a pin of a ram is immediately recognized as a silhouette shooter by those presently engaged in the rifle and pistol sports.

The scoring is simple. In a certain match, for example, forty rounds are fired at forty silhouettes for score. One point is scored by the shooter for each animal down.

For the bowhunter, twelve targets are set up: three chickens, three pigs, three turkeys and three rams. A bowhunter steps to the shooting

Competitive Archery

line with twelve arrows and shoots an arrow at each silhouette. After twelve shots he has finished a round and his score is recorded.

In a normal match the archer will shoot three rounds for a total of 36 silhouettes.

The next consideration was to develop the type of competition that would develop and improve the skills of the bowhunter. Furthermore, the program must be designed around the equipment used by the bowhunter in his hunting pursuits.

It has long been apparent that the bowhunter quickly grows weary of shooting at paper targets set are predetermined distances.

Additionally, the equipment used by the most successful target archers to shoot paper targets is generally not suited to the bowhunting sports and does little to improve a bowhunter's skills.

To represent the bowhunters' needs, the international organization has incorporated numerous features in its silhouette program to represent field conditions. This approach allows maximum utilization of bowhunting equipment and serves to improve the skills of the bowhunter. These field conditions include: a mixing of known and unknown distances, repositioning between shots, shooting time limits, life-size silhouettes, familiar animal shapes, use of bows of 40 pounds minimum pull and hunting arrows equipped with field points.

When a bowhunter steps to the line he faces twelve silhouettes (three of each series, chicken, pig, turkey and ram set at distances ranging from approximately 20 meters to 70 meters). Only four of the silhouettes are at known and marked yardages. Number 1 Chicken (25 meters), Number 1 Pig (35 meters), Number 1 Turkey (50 meters), and Number 1 Ram (65 meters). The rest of each series are placed at the discretion of the Match Director just prior to the match. Once the silhouettes are placed for a match, practice rounds are prohibited.

The bowhunter is allowed two minutes to shoot twelve arrows. Additionally, he must move laterally to the right or left between each shot. The time limitations, unmarked yardage silhouettes and the requirement for the bowhunter to move between each shot all contribute to simulate the field conditions of an international format.

The implementation of these concepts and rules requires that the target archer adjust to the bowhunting programs, rather than forcing the bowhunter to adjust his style and equipment to traditional paper target competition.

Those who are accustomed to equipment restrictions or classifications based upon equipment used will find such regulations unnecessary in international competition. In silhouette shooting it is most difficult to utilize extended stabilizers, levels, releases, etc. when the shooter

Archery

is required to move, think, and shoot 12 arrows in less than two minutes at silhouettes of different sizes and at different distances.

As if all this weren't enough, there is still one more element of silhouette shooting that has made it a growing favorite worldwide. When the silhouette is hit, something happens. It falls — it's knocked off its feet. Something entirely different from traditional target shooting.

Whether you choose to compete or just to observe an international bowhunter silhouette match, you will have to agree that finally the bowhunter has a competitive sport all his own. To successfully play the game he must learn to move, think, and shoot in a matter of seconds. And when he knocks the animal flat, those watching will immediately recognize and share in the elation of a bowhunter getting his animal.

The life-size silhouettes and the bowhunter distances may cause some of the more experienced bowhunters to approach the concept as a "piece of cake."

Nothing could be further from the truth. Duke Savora, one of the world's most accomplished big game bowhunters, feels that the game is so close to natural field conditions that a perfect score will be almost impossible. Duke is so sure that he has put up an award for the first bowhunter to score a perfect "36."

Duke says, "It is one thing to stand and shoot arrows at paper targets at known yardages, but it's something entirely different to have to move, think, and shoot all at the same time and score high marks, too."

If you try it, you may agree.

SAFETY RULES

Safety Rules

Archery is great fun and this fun should not be interrupted by accidents caused by ignoring the simple rules of safety. Accidents usually result from carelessness and thoughtlessness. Remember these rules and practice them at all times.

- Always use arrows of the right length; never one too short.
- Never use damaged bow or arrows and replace the bowstring when it becomes worn or frayed.
- Never release a bowstring without an arrow on it. "Dry-firing" is unsafe and very bad for the bow.
- Never shoot at a target too thin to stop the flight of the arrow.
- Never shoot an arrow straight up into the air.
- Always shoot at a definite target; never shoot just for the pleasure of releasing an arrow. And never fire an arrow at great distances unless you are on a safe flight range.
- Never shoot when there is even a remote chance of your arrow hitting another person.
- Wait for the "all clear" before going forward to retrieve your arrows.
- Don't attempt to retrieve them while others are shooting.
- Never shoot if there is a possibility your arrow may ricochet from the target or some other object.
- Never use another person as a target and never permit another person to hold a target for you to shoot at.
- When shooting in the woods if you cannot see around or beyond the target, always call "Timber!" before starting to shoot as a warning to others who may not have cleared the shooting line or the target area.
- Always leave one member of your party standing in front of the target while you are searching for lost arrows as a warning to others following the course. If you are alone, leave your bow on the line as a warning that its owner is in the target zone.
- Never release an arrow when you cannot see where it will land.
- Never shoot another person's bow without his permission.
- Protect your sport by being careful when shooting.

Safe Arrow Removal

Removing arrows from the target is a safe and fairly simple procedure if done properly. If not, you may injure yourself, another archer, or damage the arrows.

Place the left hand on the target face with the palm down and

Archery

the arrow lying between the index and middle finger. With the right hand, grasp the arrow close to the target face, then pull or twist it out gently and at the same angle at which it entered the target. Use the same method to remove an arrow sticking in the ground or in any other surface.

It is important to be sure that no one is close to the nock end of the arrows as they are drawn from the target. An arrow drawn from the target may strike a bystander, particularly in the eye, as the arrows are often at eye level.

The correct way to remove arrows from target.

Incorrect removal is dangerous to bystanders.

Safety Rules

Inspect Your Tackle

Before starting to shoot, examine your bow carefully, making sure the string loops are in place at the nocks, the bow is not damaged and the bowstring is not frayed. Also, check the string serving for wear.

Inspect your arrows. Look over the fletching carefully. The feathers, or vanes, should be firmly attached to the shaft. Be sure the shaft is not cracked or bent. Check the point for tightness. Never shoot an arrow without inspecting it. Never use arrows which are too short for you.

A GLOSSARY OF ARCHERY TERMS

ADDRESS THE SHOOTING LINE: To prepare to shoot.
ANCHOR POINT: A place on the face or head to which the drawing hand is brought. A necessity for accuracy.
ARMGUARD: A device, usually of leather, worn on the forearm holding the bow, to protect the arm from the snap of the bowstring.
ARROW RACK: A device for storing arrows to prevent their damage when not in use.
BACK OF BOW: The side of the bow facing away from the archer.
BELLY: The side of the bow facing the archer.
BLUNTS: Arrows having blunt rather than sharp tips. Often used for hunting small game.
BOW ARM: The arm which holds the bow.
BOWMAN: Another term for archer.
BOW RACK: A device used to hold bows when not in use.
BOWSIGHT: A mechanical device attached to the bow which enables an archer to sight directly on the target, something he cannot do with the tip of his arrow except at point-blank range.
BOWSTRING: The string used on a bow, usually made of Dacron or Kevlar.
BOWYER: A person who makes bows.
BRACED BOW: A bow which is strung and ready for shooting.
BROADHEAD: An arrowhead of metal used for hunting, using a number of extremely sharp blades.
BUTT: Any backstop for halting arrows shot at a target.
CAST: The distance a bow can propel an arrow.
CLOUT SHOOTING: Long distance shooting, usually at a circular target with a light-colored center laid out on the ground.
COCK FEATHER: The feather of an arrow which is set at right angles to the nock groove. It usually is of a different color than the other two feathers for easy identification.
COMPOSITE BOW: A bow made from two or more kinds of material.
CREEPING: Allowing the drawing hand to edge forward while aiming.
CREST: Coloring on the shaft of an arrow for identification.
CROSSBOW: A bow mounted horizontally on a gun-like stock. In early days the crossbow was considered a very powerful weapon. The heavy bow was cranked mechanically and the arrow released by pulling a trigger. The whole device is held and aimed like a rifle.
DRAW: To pull the bowstring back into shooting position.

Archery

DRAWING ARM: The arm which draws the bowstring.
DRIFT: The natural deflection of an arrow from normal flight due to the effect of wind or other outside influence.
END: Three or more arrows shot in succession.
FACE: The surface of the target.
FIELD ARROW: An arrow used in the field. It usually is longer, heavier and stronger than a target arrow.
FISTMELE: It measures the correct distance between the bow at the grip pivot point, and the bowstring.
FLETCHING: The feathers, or vanes, on an arrow.
FLETCHER: A device for placing fletch on an arrow shaft.
FLIGHT SHOOTING: A shooting contest, the object of which is to see who can shoot an arrow the greatest distance.
FLIGHT: The course of a released arrow.
GRIP: The handle of the bow where held by the archer.
GROUND QUIVER: A metal rod with a loop at the top, used to hold arrows in readiness on the ground near the archer.
HANDLE RISER: The center part of the bow.
HEAD: The tip of an arrow.
HIT: A successful shot.
HUNTING BOW: A bow made especially for hunting game.
INSTINCTIVE SHOOTING: Aiming and shooting an arrow instinctively rather than employing a mechanical aiming device or the point of aim theory.
JOINTED BOW: A two-piece bow.
KICK: The recoil of the bowstring and bow as the arrow is released.
LIMBS: The two "arms" of a bow from the handle out, which bend and give the arrow its flight motivation.
LOOSE: To shoot an arrow.
MARK: The target.
NOCK: The plastic fitting with a groove on the end of an arrow into which the bowstring is fitted. Also, the grooves at either end of the bow which hold the bowstring in place.
NOCKING POINT: That spot on the bowstring above which the arrow will be placed before drawing and shooting.
OVERBOWED: Using a bow which is too strong for the archer.
OVERDRAW: To draw the arrow back too far, so the tip of the arrow passes the belly of the bow. This is a very dangerous procedure. (Also a specific bow with extended arrow shelf.)
PETTICOAT: Any part of the target outside the outer ring. An arrow striking in the petticoat counts zero.
POINT: A unit of scoring.

Glossary

POINT-ON RANGE: The one distance from a target at which the point of aim corresponds to the center of the target.

POINT OF AIM: That point normally off the target but always in a straight line of sight with it, which enables the archer to hit his target. For short distances, it will be below the target. For long distances it will be above the target. Between the two is **point-on range** where the point of range and the target are identical. The point of aim theory is explained in the section on **Aim and Hold**.

RANGE FINDER: A device used by the archer to determine the exact distance to the target.

RELEASE: To let the bowstring slip off the fingers, sending the arrow on its way.

ROVING: A type of game or competition in which archers shoot at various objects, not knowing the exact distances to these objects.

SELF BOW: A bow made entirely of one piece of material, as compared with a composite bow.

SERVING: The thread wrapped about the bowstring to prevent the arrow or the archer's fingers from fraying the string and causing it to break.

SHAFT: That part of the arrow lying between the nock and fletching and the point.

SHOOTING TAB: A leather device which protects the fingers of the shooting hand. There are also leather gloves used for the same purpose.

SHOOTING LINE: The line upon which an archer stands while target shooting.

STRING FINGERS: The three fingers used to draw back to bowstring.

STRUNG BOW: A bow ready for shooting.

TACKLE: Archery equipment.

TARGET: The object at which the archer aims.

TARGET ARROW: An arrow, light in weight, used in shooting at the standard stationary target.

TARGET CARD: A scorecard.

TARGET FACE: The outer covering of a target on which are marked the bull's eye and the various circles.

TARGET STAND: A stand which holds the target.

TASSELL: A piece of fabric which some archers wear on their quiver or belt and use to clean arrows which become wet or soiled.

TIMBER!: In field archery, a warning which should be called out to let people in the shooting zone know that an arrow is about to be released.

UNDERBOWED: Equipped with a bow that is not as strong as the one an archer is capable of using.

VANE: A plastic feather substitute on an arrow.

WEIGHT: The amount of pull measured in pounds required to draw the bow to its full draw.

WEIGHT-IN-HAND: The actual weight of a bow.

WHITE: The outer ring of a target. An arrow striking in the white circle counts two or one points.

WINDAGE: The amount of drift of an arrow caused by the wind. Archers should allow for drift if the wind is blowing across the range.

WOBBLE: The erratic motion of an arrow in flight.

SPORTS PUBLICATIONS
by
THE ATHLETIC INSTITUTE

is backed by 48 years of promoting the advancement of sports, physical education, health, recreation and dance in America.

If you want the very best — the most up-to-date information written by leading authorities — graphic illustrations — line drawings — sequential photos and educationally sound, consider the following titles:

Archery	Pathfinder (Backpacking)
Badminton	Power Volleyball, The Woman's Game
Basketball	Basketball, The Woman's Game
On The Lesson Tee	Health Care and the Female Athlete
Run America	A Manual for Women's Self-Defense
Soccer	Modern Women's Gymnastics
Tennis Your Way	Softball, Fast and Slo Pitch
Racquetball 1-2-3	Touch and Flag Football Rules
Modern Athletic Training	Track & Field for Men and Women

Coaches Edition:
Youth League Baseball
Youth League Basketball
Youth League Football
Youth League Ice Hockey
Youth League Soccer
Youth League Softball
Youth League Wrestling

For Information On Obtaining These Books Write To:
The Athletic Institute
Publications Department
200 Castlewood Drive
North Palm Beach, FL 33408